The Social Conscience of Business

THE M. L. SEIDMAN MEMORIAL
TOWN HALL LECTURE SERIES

MEMPHIS STATE UNIVERSITY

The M. L. Seidman Memorial Town Hall Lecture Series was established by P. K. Seidman in memory of his late brother, M. L. Seidman, founder of the firm Seidman and Seidman, Certified Public Accountants.

Publication of this eighth Series of Seidman Lectures was made possible by a gift from Mr. P. K. Seidman to the Memphis State University Press.

The M. L. Seidman Memorial Town Hall Lecture Series

1966-67   *Financial Policies in Transition*
           edited by Dr. Thomas O. Depperschmidt

1967-68   *The USSR in Today's World*
           edited by Dr. Festus Justin Viser

1968-69   *The News Media — A Service and a Force*
           edited by Dr. Festus Justin Viser

1969-70   *Taxation — Dollars and Sense*
           edited by Dr. Festus Justin Viser

1970-71   *The University in Transition*
           edited by Dr. Festus Justin Viser

1971-72   *China's Open Wall*
           edited by Dr. Festus Justin Viser

1972-73   *Crime and Justice*
           edited by Dr. Festus Justin Viser

The Social Conscience of Business

edited by Phineas J. Sparer

MEMPHIS STATE UNIVERSITY PRESS   1974

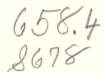

Library of Congress Cataloging in Publication Data

The social conscience of business.

(The M. L. Seidman memorial town hall lecture series,
1973-74) *74-8900*
CONTENTS: Nathan, R. R. Competition and conscience in
American business community. —Hodges, L. H. The responsibility
of American business toward the community. —Metz, R. The forgotten individual: 30-million investors.
1. Industry — Social aspects — United States — Addresses,
essays, lectures. I. Sparer, Phineas J., comp. II. Series.
HD60.5.U5S63   658.4'08   74-14909

ISBN 0 - 87870 - 023 - 4

Contents

Coordinating Committee

FESTUS J. VISER, Director
 Professor of Economics
 Memphis State University

ROBERT T. GARNETT, Assistant Director
 Program Coordinator for
 Public Service and Continuing Education
 Memphis State University

FRANK R. AHLGREN
 Retired Editor
 Memphis Commercial Appeal

JERRY N. BOONE
 Vice President for Academic Affairs
 Memphis State University

FRED P. COOK
 Vice President and Station Manager
 WREC AM-FM Radio Station

KURT F. FLEXNER
 Chairman, Department of Economics
 Memphis State University

MRS. ROLAND H. MYERS
 Hostess, "Challenge To Read"
 WREC Radio

ABE PLOUGH
 Chairman of the Board
 Plough, Inc.

P. K. SEIDMAN
 Partner
 Seidman and Seidman CPA

BRUCE A. SPACEK
 Partner
 Seidman and Seidman CPA

PHINEAS J. SPARER
 Emeritus Professor
 College of Medicine
 University of Tennessee

The Social Conscience of Business

Preface

If history deals with the scope and complexities of the dynamic interaction of two major life forces — the extrinsic force of circumstances and the intrinsic force of human character — then the following pages portray a critical segment of contemporary American life involving the nature of business and the character of man.

It is interesting to note that the Coordinating Committee of the M. L. Seidman Town Hall Lectures sponsored by Memphis State University chose The Social Conscience of Business as the theme for the 1973-1974 series.

For this venture, to consider the relevance and prevalence of the social conscience of business in our contemporary society, the Committee was fortunate to select three outstanding and worthy spokesmen: the economist Robert R. Nathan; former Secretary of Commerce, Luther H. Hodges; and The New York Times columnist, Robert R. Metz. Each of them from his own area of expertise and experience articulated competently and clearly the problems and obligations of business in our society.

In the light of history, classical economics acknowledged business to be acting in a socially responsible way if it strived to maximize profits by efficiently utilizing available resources in providing the goods and services that people wanted at market prices. However, the current concept of social responsibility has been extended and often referred to as the social conscience of business, which involves two chief aspects: the conscience of the business organization per se; and the conscience of significant individuals within it. This duality, particularly applicable to large corporations, encompasses activities pertinent to the restricted primary aim of the private enterprise system towards maximizing the yield of profit but this is not the only legitimate demand of business and of the individuals within it. Profit, the life-blood of business, is a most potent incentive to economic pursuit and advancement, and extended functions toward social welfare. Also, consonant with the principal of laissez-faire, the traditional economic notion prevails that by pursuing their own interests, the corporation and its individuals thereby pursue the interests of the public.

In point of fact, the extraordinary power-structure of our contemporary society is confronted with the ever changing activities and policies that are becoming the bases of great concern and that are portending a new era of progressive change in the social conscience of business. The concept of laissez-faire was developed at a time when business enterprises were actually very small and hence incapable of immoderate power in the marketplace or elsewhere. Since the industrial revolution, however, corporations experienced a period of rapid technological development augmented with increased laissez-faire tendencies. By virtue of those factors, corporations have grown to tremendous size and have become capable of exerting immense power not only in the marketplace but also in the body politic as well as in other places.

New policies and concomitant salutary practices are already affecting contemporary business rationale and its broadening intrinsic and extrinsic social performance. New valuations, along with their emergent responsibilities are actually reflected in a new corporate image, shaping present and future directions and activities in various relevant sectors of our life-style — especially in more just employee relations including maintenance of their health and prevention of illness, in correction of certain inequities, in extension of civil rights, in promotion of educational, recreational, and rehabilitative programs, and in other new type activities. But as yet, there is no generally accepted criterion or dogma by which the social conscience of business can be determined or measured.

It is a matter of economic history that the laissez-faire doctrine, with paramount emphasis on maximum "personal interest" as serving maximum social benefit, had its origin at the end of the 17th century and beginning of the 18th century in protest to excessive restrictions and regulations of commerce or trade by the then extant state of affairs. According to one of its chief proponents, Mercier de la Riviere, the doctrine of laissez-faire held that "Personal interest compels each man vigorously and continuously to perfect and to multiply the things he seeks to sell. He thus enlarges the mass of pleasures other men can produce for him in exchange. The world thus advances of itself." Apparently, there is pivotal faith in the power of uncontrolled individualism acting to produce the social good by summation of all individual action and the caveat "laissez-faire, laissez passer", the shiboleth of those who champion and cherish naturally free and unregulated economy to "let things be the way they will".

In its characteristic form that creed attained its peak about 100 years ago but its influence still continues in some guise, to some extent, in contemporary philosophical and political ideologies as well as, indeed, in the area of economics, particularly in that of big business.

Milton Friedman, the University of Chicago economist, still persists with the classical economists in his maintaining that " . . . there is one and only one social responsibility of business — to use its resources and engage in activities designed to increase profits so long as it stays within the rules of the game, which is to say, engages in open and free competition, without deception or fraud . . . Few trends could so thoroughly undermine the very foundations

of our free society as the acceptance by corporate officials
of a social responsibility other than to make as much money
for their stockholders as possible."

On the other hand, in a study authorized by the
Federal Council of Churches in 1949, R. M. MacIver, Professor Emeritus of Political Philosophy and Sociology,
Columbia University writes partly as follows about the
Government and the Goals of Economic Activity: "The
means to many of the goals of living may be sought by
enlisting for the purpose in hand either the mechanism of
government or the mechanism of the market. One or the
other way or some combination of both may be chosen, and
the particular choice is nearly always a matter of contro-
versy . . . we should beware of arguments that sweepingly
prognosticate the direct consequences for new intervention
by government in economic affairs and denounce any
change, no matter what its manifest benefit, as heralding
"socialism", "communism", "the servile society", "the road
to serfdom" or what not. Every modern society, at least
outside of the Soviet block, is sociocapitalistic, some kind
of combination of the economic way and the political way.
It is inevitable that it should be so."

Now some biographical notes and comments appropos
of the three selected spokesmen in the lecture series.

The economist Robert R. Nathan, President of the firm
of consultant economists bearing his name, in Washington,
D.C., was born in Dayton, Ohio, in 1908. He received the
B. S. degree in Economics from the University of Pennsyl-
vania in 1931 where he was Research Assistant for a couple
of years. He then attended Georgetown University, where
in 1933 he received the M. A. in Economics and the LL.B.
in 1938. He served the Department of Commerce as an
economist in the Bureau of Foreign and Domestic Commerce for four years and as the Chief of the National In-

come Division for another four years. He has been Economic Adviser to many countries, including France, Burma, Republic of Korea, Puerto Rico, Israel, Ghana, Iran, and Nigeria. He also held some other government positions: Deputy Director, Office of War Mobilization and Reconversion in 1945; and previously, Chairman of the Planning Committee, War Production, 1942-1943; and Chief, Requirements Division, Defense Advisory Commission and Office of Production Management in 1940. Mr. Nathan has contributed his services to several political and professional associations and he has written a number of articles, including *National Income* and *Mobilizing for Abundance.* He has also co-authored *Palestine, Problem and Promise* and *A National Wage Policy for 1947.*

Because of his wide experience in government affairs, Mr. Nathan expanded his top *Competition and Conscience In the American Business Community* to include the role of the government in determining economic policies. He strongly believes in our private enterprise system and considers the challenge to be that of achieving appropriate balances between both public and private responsibilities and functions rather than regarding either the public or private extreme as necessary or feasible; and he underscores the needs of our economy to be broader and better competition combined with excellence of conscience in guiding citizen actions towards better ways of living that the interplay of a public-private mix can achieve.

Luther H. Hodges, a former U. S. Secretary of Commerce in the administration of both Presidents Kennedy and Johnson, was born in Pittsburgh, Virginia, in 1898. He earned the B.A. degree at the University of North Carolina in 1919 and he has been the recipient of several honorary degrees from other universities. He was in active business with a large textile corporation for over 30 years followed by administrative public service. In 1950 he was appointed Head of Industry Division, Economic Cooperation Administration in West Germany and in 1951 became consultant to U. S. Department of State on International Management Conference. Upon the death of the Governor, Mr. Hodges succeeded to the Governorship of North Carolina in 1954 and two years later was elected to a 4-year term as Governor. He currently serves on several corporate boards, including chairman of the Board of Financial Consultants International, S. A. in Brussels, Belgium. Mr. Hodges is the author of the book *The Business Conscience,* with the royalties therefrom assigned to the United Negro College Fund (U. S. A.) and to the Methodist Colleges of North Carolina. Mr. Hodges chose *The Responsibility of American Business Toward the Community* for his forum topic. In exploring this viewpoint, he probes deep into perplexing business problems, relating them to moral problems and he sympathetically and effectively points out that although a degree of government regulation is required in many aspects of business enterprise and competition, it is essential that industry lead rather than be led, in voluntary programs to benefit the community. He thus agrees with the public-private mix emphasized by Mr. Nathan. There is great need, according to Mr. Hodges' hard-earned view, for the United States to demonstrate how well an ethically-based economic system can function and contribute to the well-being of the people in the community as well as to people elsewhere in the world.

Robert R. Metz, a New York Times daily columnist, specializing in financial and business subjects, was born in Richmond Hill, New York in 1929; and he graduated from Wesleyan University, Connecticut in 1951, with the B.A. degree. In the same year, he started as a New York Times copy boy, subsequently succeeding to be Assistant News

Editor and News Editor; and also President and Editor in 1972 of The Newspaper Enterprise Association. His daily column "Market Place", on small business enterprises, has appeared in the financial section of The Times five days a week since 1966 and his column was the winner of the coveted Loeb Award in Journalism last year for a series on major slides in stock prices in single trades — specifically, Wrigley's 40-point drop. He has become a popular lecturer on financial topics and has made numerous appearances on radio and television shows in connection with books he has authored: "How to Shake the Money Tree", "Franchising: How to Select a Business of Your Own", and a third book, "The Tax Conscious Investor".

Mr. Metz captioned his thesis *The Forgotten Individual: 30-Million Investors*. He depicts a candid but sordid picture of the stock market's dishonorable dealings in so far as some of the 30-million individual investors are concerned, accounting for their loss of faith and financial undoing. He suggests that the entire system suffers when sharp practice occurs and he therefore further suggests that it is proper for the businessman to actively seek better laws to prevent the rip-off of the individual investor and to restore a greater measure of faith to our system by assuring the customer that his ability to trade shares will not be impaired by weakness or failure of his broker, and by other safeguards to the customer, e.g. as depositors in banks who are protected by federal deposit insurance.

Mr. Metz deplores, nay, condemns those businessmen who regard their role in the light that "If it is profitable and we can get away with it, then it must be right." Such attitude, he considers dangerous and outrageous especially when it is evidenced in high-ranking businessmen, distinguished-looking, gifted and determined corporate muggers who deftly plot the individual investors ruin and who use the very laws that are designed to protect shareholders to carry out such chicanery. Mr. Metz cites a number of instances to illustrate his claim that the moral tone of business is low, indeed, even with giant corporations that do not mind promoting a dishonest message, so long as there is no way to hold the corporation legally responsible. It is his judgement that corporations have neglected to meet their responsibilities as citizens and are not yet sufficiently socially conscientious — not yet governed by the dictates of conscience.

Multiple thanks are due many participants who made this venture successful. First, to Memphis State University for its continued encouraging sponsorship and to several of its staff members for the substantial contributions of their time and talent. Then to the Coordinating Committee members who always pursued their tasks ardently and assiduously. Also, to Mrs. Reva Cook for her excellent publicity. And above all, a debt of profound gratitude to Mr. P. K. Seidman for his practical support of the lecture forum as a fraternal devotion to the late M. L. Seidman, whom the annual Town Hall Lecture Series memorialize, thereby serving to stimulate and illuminate contemporary thought on the University campus as well as in the Memphis community.

Phineas J. Sparer
June, 1974

"Competition and Conscience in the American
Business Community"

Lecture One

by Robert R. Nathan

Perhaps the title of this lecture should be expanded to include the role of government in determining economic policies. One of the three principal determinants in our economic life is provided by competition and the market place. Conscience and performance of entrepreneurs and managers serve as a second important contributing factor. Over the years the part played by government has increasingly been respected and recognized as a vital economic force.

I believe in our free enterprise system and regard it as the best that man has evolved. However, it has its weaknesses along with its strengths. If we are to enhance its strong points and correct the system's faults, we must better understand how the whole system works, evaluate its successes and failures objectively, and be willing to explore and even experiment with innovative policies and practices.

The American economy is a mixed as well as a complex economy. It is not capitalism in the traditional sense, although some present-day liberals believe it retains most of the harsh features of laissez-faire. Definitely it is not socialism, despite the views expressed around the National Association of Manufacturers that all those New Deal, Fair Deal, New Society, and Great Society programs were pure unadulterated socialism if not quite communist in character.

A notable feature is that there is little public ownership of *productive* resources in the United States, although much public policy shapes the economy and affects input and the distribution of output. Most enterprises are privately owned and there are few cooperatives, but much of the private sector does not and never did perform in line with competitive and free market theories. References to the "good old days" conjure fantasies of much vigorous competition that never did exist. The growth in scale of enterprises and conglomerates and multinational corporations give some credence to the idea that competition is not as great as it was and far less than what we are often told it was.

Highly polarized descriptions and judgments about the nature of our economy have limited validity. It certainly is neither all free nor all regulated and, equally true, it is not all good nor all bad. Government inroads have not undermined the dominant and profit-yielding role of business in the free enterprise system. Through government policies and practices considerable progress has been made in overcoming the more severe human environmental and wasteful consequences of the "let nature take its course" approach.

A brief review of economic progress over the last half century and the up-to-date performance show impressive evidence of substantial and pervasive improvement. Yet, there are continuing serious deficiencies in the functioning of our economy. A review will be useful in putting future problems and policies in proper perspective.

In 1924, just 50 years ago, this country was going through a minor recession following the recovery from the short but severe post-war deflation in 1921. There was a recession in 1927, and then came the Great Depression starting in 1929 and bottoming out in 1932 and early 1933. That was a disaster of major dimensions which will forever be inscribed in big black letters in our economic history.

The outstanding economic accomplishment in American economic history was the taming of the business cycle after the Great Depression. The halting and incomplete but still impressive recovery record of the 1930's and the successful mobilization of resources for World War II provided sufficient experience and confidence to formulate and adopt the Employment Act of 1946.

The word *taming* is used advisedly because we are still experiencing recurring recessions. However, an overwhelming proportion of economists agree we need not and will not ever have another major depression. The American people have concluded that we need not let nature take its course, that we can moderate booms and busts, and that we will never again resign ourselves to a severe depression. We no longer believe in the inevitability of major business cycles or that they are inherent ingredients of the free enterprise system. This determination and confidence is now imbedded in our solid performance.

The Employment Act of 1946 represents a notable milestone in American economic policy. For the first time the United States Government committed itself to the maintenance of high levels of production, income, and employment. In the nearly three decades since that law was enacted we have never in any calendar year suffered a drop of more than 2 percent in total production. Unemployment has not averaged above 7 percent in any year since World War II. That is remarkable compared with the depression depths of 1932 when one out of four persons in the labor force was totally unemployed. Millions of others were employed only part time. The real gross national product dropped by nearly one-third from 1929 to 1933.

The prestigious National Bureau of Economic Research has defined a recession as a drop in total output in two successive calendar quarters. When President Nixon decreed in his 1974 State of the Union speech that there would not be a recession in 1974 he did not refer to any definition. His chief economic adviser promptly gave the President an out by indicating that something more substantial than just declines in real output in two successive quarters may be preferable for defining a recession.

Be that as it may, our performance standards are certainly higher than they used to be. We now become deeply troubled over minor drops in output and slight increases in unemployment. Some economists even want to define cessations in growth as recessions. It is different from the old days when booms and busts were largely taken for granted.

Greatly reduced fluctuations in economic activity represent only one of the many improvements over the last half century. Full employment eases social and economic hardships but it does not by any means solve all or perhaps most of them. It does make solutions more manageable.

A broad range of policies and actions have been adopted to insulate individual and family lives from hardships associated with the capitalist system but there is much yet to be done. Millions of American citizens still suffer privation, insecurity and hardships amidst abundance in this affluent society. There is inadequate provision for reasonably minimum sharing even though remarkable progress has been made.

It is hard today to realize that prior to the late 1930's

there was no overall social security system in the United States. There was no national old age pension program. There were no nationwide unemployment insurance provisions and no standards in that regard and no national categorical assistance measures.

Today nearly 20 million elderly Americans receive about $40 billion in assured retirement income each year because of the Federal old age pension program. Additional millions get billions in survivor and disability benefits. Millions get public assistance, unemployment compensation, and help through other supportive measures. True, the level of most benefits is too low even for minimum security, but compared with conditions in the '20's and the '30's the contribution to the well-being of the American people made by the social security has been most impressive. Cash benefits under public social insurance and related programs is approaching $100 billion a year and that is not a minor sum by any standard.

A broad catalogue of other reforms was introduced or initiated in the 1930's. Minimum wages have contributed materially to raising living standards for the working poor. Today, with a minimum wage of $1.60 an hour and a level of perhaps $2.20 in the offing, it is startling to recall that the first minimum wage in the late '30's was 25 cents an hour. Time-and-a-half pay for overtime work is also a product of the Fair Labor Standards Act of the late '30's. Legislation assuring workers the right to bargain collectively and thereby improve the terms of compensation and conditions of work has had, also, a major positive impact on the well-being of employees.

Many conservatives, including neo-classical economists, bitterly fought all of those reforms. They have gradually but grudgingly accepted them as additions that are here to stay and possible to live with. But, resistance to every proposed further improvement still continues.

It is not only in the laws affecting income and the workers where we have made tremendous progress. Regulations requiring truth in floating new securities and prevention of abuses in security and commodity transactions have enhanced the economic security of the American people. Banking deposit insurance was a tremendous step forward. Few people who lived through the Great Depression in the early '30's will ever forget the havoc wrought by bank failures across this country that wiped out lifetime savings of millions of American families. Banks and savings and loan associations still fail occasionally, but deposit insurance protects the deposits up to designated amounts. The entire mortgage market was revolutionized through mortgage insurance and the widespread introduction of the amortization principle in mortgages on housing.

Unfortunately, progress made in the more recent war on poverty and in urban redevelopment and the rehabilitation of other distressed areas has been less marked. We still have terrible slums with rat-infested substandard houses. We still have rural regions where small farmers barely eke out an existence. Discrimination and prejudice on grounds of minority, sex, religious, and age groupings still prevail. The income and employment status of blacks have improved greatly but there is still no real equality of opportunity.

As our society becomes more affluent its deficiencies and the gaps between the haves and the have-nots become increasingly untenable. For example, a half century ago there was little talk about *the* poverty problem in the United States — and not because people did not suffer from hunger, poor housing, scant clothing, limited health services, little education, and other manifestations of poverty. President Franklin Delano Roosevelt spoke of the "ill-fed, the ill-housed, and the ill-clothed," but there was no clamor for an all-out war on poverty or an income maintenance program or a negative income tax.

There was almost universal poverty, or at least poverty among such an overwhelming portion of the population that it was accepted as a common and permanent characteristic of our society. Even in the booming days of the 1920's, when jobs were plentiful, most Americans were poor. It is only when a sizable portion of the population moves into the middle and upper income levels that the gaps become more apparent and more difficult to accept.

As children of the poor get a better education and find improved employment opportunities we may well be able to break the vicious cycle of poverty begetting poverty. A slow and uneven upgrading process is taking place. A great many do escape the grinding hardship and hopelessness of real poverty and we no longer accept the view that "the poor will always be poor," let alone "the poor will always be with us." Nevertheless, this breaking out of the poverty cycle makes those who are left behind more evident sufferers in the midst of plenty.

Even though we have pretty much tamed the business cycle, we still have costly recessions and underemployment. Six percent unemployment is much better than 25 percent of the labor force being idle but it represents failure compared with the 3.5 percent in the late 1960's. Those who lose their jobs recoup only part of their income through unemployment compensation and then for only a limited time. They get hurt through no fault of their own and the nation loses the goods and services that would otherwise be produced. Had full employment persisted from 1970 through 1973 we would have produced about $150 billion more than we did. Such a waste is not to be taken lightly.

We also have a long way to go in learning how to cope with the problems of inflation. Historically, inflation was largely associated with booms and wars. After a half decade of remarkable price stability from 1960 to 1965, our country entered on a worsening course and now on serious inflation. It was set off by the coincidence of three independent factors that converged within a short period of time, namely: (a) economic expansion that began to take effect in 1965 as a result of the 1964 tax cut; (b) large military orders beginning in 1965 associated with the Vietnam War; and (c) sharp curtailment of agricultural intories due to droughts abroad, especially in India, in 1965. The inflation has steadily worsened. The year 1974 will see the worst rate of inflation in our country since the first six months of the Korean War. The so-called "war on inflation" is a failure of disastrous proportions.

Overall monetary and fiscal policies have not done the job. In fact they are becoming less and less effective as the spiral of inflation gains its own pernicious momentum. Economists in the Nixon administration keep contending that it would have been much worse but for fiscal and monetary restraints. But the 1970-71 recession did not restore relative price stability and there is litle prospect that the 1974 business contraction will make any dent whatsoever in the upward surge of prices. Few say it openly, but Nixon administration economists believe much higher levels and longer duration of unemployment will be needed to get back to reasonable price stability. Theirs is a bankruptcy of practical ideas and policies.

The blame for inflation placed on labor has abated because it would be so patently false. Labor has exercised remarkable restraint in wage demands for some years. In fact, labor has been victimized by the inflation and the buying power of workers' incomes actually declined in 1973.

Direct controls helped slow inflation in late 1971 and in 1972 but controls became less and less effective after a series of mistakes, inept management and reliance on rhetoric and mirrors rather than serious enforcement controls. Some, including myself, believe that those responsible for controls have botched them as badly as could have been done by any group which designedly set out to discredit controls. They plead *nolo contendere* on the grounds that controls undermine the efficient allocation of resources, ignoring the bad effects of continuing and worsening inflation on resource allocation.

All this is regrettable, because too many leaders in this country have resigned themselves to inflation and are now concentrating on ways and means of living with inflation rather than ways and means of fighting inflation and reestablishing price stability. Obfuscation and even misrepresentation by officials of economic policies and economic prospects have spread an aura of hopelessness. It is more than just a lack of leadership from which the nation's economy is suffering. It is a matter of *bad leadership, bad policies* and *lack of forthrightness.* We are suffering from a Watergate-type of economics.

We seem to have lost ground in many equity areas. Federal income tax rates have been reduced substantially on a number of occasions over the past couple of decades. The incidence of Federal income taxes at the higher levels has tended to fall relative to the burden at the lower income levels, thus reducing the progressivity of these taxes from what they would have been without the cuts. No one would have believed a decade ago that top rates on earned income would be reduced to 50 percent, which is where they now are. In the name of tax reform, rates have been cut and the incidence reduced at the top. Little or nothing has been done about eliminating loopholes. The nation needs protection from more such tax reforms!

Also, Federal taxes have dropped as the ratio of total public revenues, with county, state and local taxes rising not only rapidly in dollar terms, but also relative to Federal taxes sense. There has been a modest rise in state income taxes but most state revenues still come from sales and property taxes, which tend to take a larger portion of the low income dollar than they do from higher incomes.

Payroll taxes have risen tremendously and these are the most regressive of all taxes, falling much more heavily on the lower income groups than they do on the higher income levels. Surely, some portion of social security financing ought to be provided from general revenues. The shifting total tax burden is so inequitable as to invite tax revolts.

Conservation is another important problem and we have made very little headway toward its solution. We are at last becoming a little conscious of the tremendous rate at which critical natural resources are being chewed up in a mad race for growth which literally threatens to destroy growth. But, there is a big lag between awareness and action. Growth in and of itself is not necessarily bad. In fact, economic growth can make resources available to achieve many of the worthy objectives which mankind seeks to fulfill. Production can grow without eroding our resource base if we program scarce supplies intelligently.

Likewise, the way in which expanding output is distributed and used is as important as growth in and of itself. Unfortunately, we have not done well in the distribution of our abundance. We have continued — and if anything simultaneously have intensified — the trickle down process of the poor scrambling for left-overs while the affluent live more wastefully and ostentatiously. Perhaps the energy crisis and the threat of other shortages will make us much more conscious that supplies of fuel as well as other materials are finite and that we will endanger our posterity if we do not mend our ways.

Another long neglected problem concerns our precious environment. We are in danger of polluting our air and our water, our food and our farms, our cities and our seashores, our hearing capabilities and our recreational resources. Disregard for conservation has in and of itself been a contributing factor to the deteriorating environment. Now that the energy crisis has hit us hard, the pressure is consequently strong to abandon what little progress has been made toward preventing further environmental deterioration. We seem bent on pursuing irresponsible practices that will make it impossible for the next generation to have essential materials, clean air, clean water and other vital requirements for survival. We blindly resist even slight sacrifices in the rate of increase in our standard of living today as a small price for a safer and better tomorrow.

A different area where economic problems ahead threaten to be increasingly difficult and solutions more elusive concerns international trade and monetary arrangements. For a couple of decades after World War II the United States provided constructive and world-oriented economic leadership. We set an example in reducing tariffs when others agreed to follow suit and to eliminate or curtail quotas and other barriers to trade among the nations. We were generous in providing former allies and enemies with capital assistance for economic rehabilitation. We made available tens of billions of dollars worth of technical assistance and capital facilities and surplus foods through grants and loans to the less developed countries. Internationally and regionally, we supported financial and developmental institutions. We cooperated in developing international monetary mechanisms that would enhance exchange rate stability. We encouraged the flow of capital. Many nations that could well afford to do so did not reciprocate and we saw much of our gold reserves go abroad and huge dollar balances were built up in other nations. Thereby, the dollar weakened and our trade situation deteriorated.

For the first time in more than a generation there is danger that the United States may become protectionist and once again pursue the divisive policies of higher tariffs and trade restraints. A combination of improved productivity and efficiency in other industrial countries and in some of the rapidly advancing nations, coupled with the inflation here in the United States, resulted in a deteriorating trade balance for us and our first trade deficit in decades. Then two devaluations of the dollar and multiple revaluations of the Japanese yen and the German Deutschmark brought about considerable improvement in America's trade balance and balance of payments in 1973. However, our improved trade and payments situation was paralleled by reduced trade surpluses in Japan and Germany and some other western European countries. There was grumbling but no serious threat of a trade war until the energy crisis hit with an explosive force. Now the scramble is jungle-like among the fuel and other material-importing nations in trying to protect their trade patterns, their exchange rates and reserves and their high rates of economic growth. We have a bad situation in which free world leadership is desparately needed and our current posture hardly fits that critical need.

These extended observations on both achieved progress and persistent problems, especially with respect to the latter, might well raise questions as to how all this is relevant to the title, namely, "Competition and Conscience in the American Business Community." There is a direct relationship, nevertheless, because the solution of our difficult and nagging economic problems will depend on how our economic system functions, how the private sector contributes to the solution of those problems, and how the government participates in economic policies and activities. Hard and objective evaluations are needed on *how well or how badly* we have done over the long term as well as in the recent past and present if we are going to set a more successful course for the future. Can we rely largely or increasingly on the competitive role of American business — in meeting the challenges ahead? Can or should business management temper its profit maximizing drive with actions that derive from conscience and involve concern about social, ethical, cultural, and political as well as economic deficiencies? Further, what can be expected of the American businessman, not only in the terms of his running a business but also in his role as a citizen? Will we need a change in the relative mix of public and private responsibilities? What can be done to reduce the costs of the economy's inadequate performance and still preserve the great and enduring benefits that flow from competition and free enterprise?

In seeking answers to the many economic problems we face, we should not expect easy and costless solutions. Alternatives will not be simple to identify or define. Insofar as business itself is concerned, there will seldom be alternative choices between competition on the one hand and conscience on the other. These are put into juxtaposition largely because there are widely divergent views on the degree of reliance we can or should place on competition

and on conscience in fulfilling national or pro-social objectives.

The "let nature take its course" traditional or classical
school of economists espouse the thesis that if only the
free enterprise system were not interfered with and if competition were unfettered from government interference, the
millenium would soon be reached and all our problems
would vanish like the proverbial dew before the rising
sun. They believe that competition is the beginning and the
summum bonum of economic life. They think the economic
difficulties of the United States are largely attributable to
some mysterious forces turned loose by evilness or simple-
mindedness. This may be a slight exaggeration of the attitudes of President Nixon's top economists but it isn't too
farfetched.

There are others who take the very opposite view,
namely, that competition is just an illusion because tough
competition doesn't exist in most industries or that even
where it does prevail, it fails to fully serve the needs of
our society. They argue strongly that the government must
not just establish some rules of fair play and then step aside
and let the free market carry on, but that there must be a
continuing important place in the economic scheme for
public participation through government action. Of course,
the degree and nature of government's role is subject to a
wide spectrum of judgments. Before considering this government role let us examine the roles of competition and
conscience.

Most American economists, including myself, strongly
support the economic system under which we live and
operate, and most of us favor the principles and practices
associated with vigorous and fair competition. But very
often we are critical of the limited degree of real competition and of the way in which competition works. The

bitter truth is that we have far from real competition in most sectors of our economy. The exceptions do not apply only to public utilities and other regulated monopolies. The degree of competition varies greatly from one sector to another, but there are very few fields of economic endeavor where one can say that competition is truly descriptive of the way in which the sector functions.

Perhaps the most competitive field is retail trade, and yet even here one finds pressures in many states for fair trade laws which permit the maintenance of prices as determined by manufacturers. Competition is vigorous in most of the service areas, but in many of the professions, including medicine and law, there are so many professional mysticisms, technical terms and confusing functions as to raise grave doubts of the effectiveness of communication in any competition. Certainly, much of this competition is not focused on prices.

What is most disturbing is the degree of administered pricing and "follow-the-leader" practices in so many industries. I am reminded of a hearing conducted many years ago before a Senate Committee chaired by the late Estes Kefauver of this state. Kefauver was asking an official of one of the large steel companies why the companies always changed their prices by the exact number dollars and cents per ton as did the price leader of the industry. He was told that this practice was followed to "keep competitive." This is the kind of rationalizing that prevails in a great many industries where price competition is professed in word but frowned upon in practice. One gets cynical listening to officials in the administered price industries waving the flag for free enterprise, when any critical observer knows it is a phony posture.

We need to strengthen and preserve true competition, to stimulate it to the maximum extent possible. But we must not delude ourselves into believing that competition, and especially the discipline of the marketplace, assuming it could be effectively achieved, would provide the solutions to all our economic problems, as so many of the laissez-faire economists seem to think.

Competition did not prevent us from having business cycles in the long span of most of our economic history. Competition did not prevent hardships to the unemployed. Competition did not serve to eliminate racial prejudices and biases in jobs and entrepreneurial opportunities. Competition did not prevent us from despoiling our environment and from eroding our resource base. Competition did not bring reasonably high levels of employment and price stability. Competition did not preserve mass transit and efficient use of transit fuel. Competition did not prevent the energy crisis, and in fact it probably aggravated the wasteful use of scarce resources. Competition did not contribute to the achievement of reasonable price stability without resort to the untenable weapons of recession and unemployment. History records that competition did not assure pure foods and clean restaurants and the elimination of child labor and a host of other practices we abhor today.

Yet, truly, competition does have an important role to play in the effective functioning of our free enterprise system, and we should strive to preserve as much competition as possible. But it is going to be neither as universally practiced nor as vigorously pursued as theorists would have us expect or believe. Nor is it going to perform the miracles promised by its ardent devotees. Nor will it preclude the need for governmental policies designed to make for the optimum performance of our economy and for equity and resource conservation and a healthy environment and other worthy over-riding considerations. In fact governmental intervention is needed to prevent the elimination of competition through monopolistic practices. Achieving more vigorous competition is not a highly feasible goal. Every time the government fights monopolistic practices in any industry, the resistance is overwhelming. Legal loopholes are discovered more rapidly and more pervasively than improvements in the law and in attempts to enforce the law. Those very individuals who espouse competition as the way to achieve the millennium are the very ones who, more often than not, practice monopoly and restraint of trade and dare term antitrust prosecutions as persecutions.

My emphasis on the limitations of competition should not be interpreted as either opposition to the competitive system or a lack of belief in a great many values flowing from real competition. In the attempt to emphasize that competition has been oversold as the solution to every economic problem I do not want to leave the thought that we can do without competition. That would be very costly because without competition we would soon have a substantially different economic system, and the losses of freedom and efficiency and productivity would far exceed, in my judgment, whatever we might gain in changing to another system. Rather, we should strengthen competitive forces and pursue public policies that will assure the maximum benefits from competition and also supplement those benefits through constructive governmental actions.

The question then presents itself as to what the role of the businessman should be, and what his conscience can or should contribute to our national goals and objectives. Here, it seems to me, we must distinguish entrepreneurs and managers in the business community as *businessmen and business leaders on the one hand, and as citizens on the other*. It is not easy to make this distinction in practice because business leaders are in positions to exercise considerable power and authority in the community, not just with respect to business matters but with respect to social, political, religious, philanthropic, and general community affairs. The very fact that they play important roles and are potent leaders makes it urgent for us to evaluate carefully the role of the businessman in the American scene.

I agree with the school of thought that, in running his business, the businessman should not be philanthropic but should seek profits. He should not try to decide what is good for his suppliers and workers and customers but should pay as little as he can for goods and services and sell for as much as he can competitively and make as large a profit as his competitive position permits. Job security for each employee is not his sole responsibility but he should be assured by governmental policies on unemployment compensation, training and retraining and on the protected bargaining between management and unions. He should be innovative and seek high productivity and efficiency. Yes, as a businessman, he should behave in partisan pursuit of his business interests and enterprise.

But as a citizen as well as a businessman he should, in good conscience, follow humane codes of decency, honesty and fair play. He should not falsely describe his products or services. He should not cheat suppliers and workers and customers through misrepresentation. Tough competition does not require dishonesty, nor does it entail neglect of quality and safety of product, or disregard for the well-being of plant and office workers, or disobedience of laws, or conspiring with competitors to engage in monopolistic practices, or violating common propriety.

In essence, the businessman should seek to be a successful profit-maker and a builder of a strong and expanding enterprise. The influence of his conscience should constantly stop him from cheating and abusing his power or engaging in sharp practices that are illegal or unethical. But his conscience should not make him into a do-gooder, or wrong-doer, as a businessman.

The conscience of the man in business should, however, be just as potent as any other person's when it comes to exercising rights and responsibilities as a citizen. The businessman not only has power on his own because of his economic role in our society but also because many citizens recognize and respect that power. Many persons may dislike business leaders and even distrust them but still know that business leaders acquire prestige and can exercise more influence than average citizens. Wealth and high income are status symbols whether the status is used for good or evil. So, the businessman is a prominent citizen and he can be an important one.

The problem is that few persons can compartmentalize their lives, distinguish their interests in different functions and reckon with them justly. A conservative businessman is likely to be conservative politically. A tense and driving business executive is not likely to be a relaxed and "brothers-keeper" kind of neighbor. Yet, many highly cost-conscious business executives are highly philanthropic in community undertakings. Some businessmen will drive very hard bargains with unions, but will cooperate willingly with workers and labor leaders in civic activities.

It is largely because top business executives have prestige in the community that we hope their consciences would make them more active and more creditable and more influential citizens. And as citizens it might be hoped that they would not all work together in ways that would set off the businessman citizen clique against other citizen groups. Maybe that is too much to expect because human behavior is to some extent a product of the daily environment, and the citizen who is in his business all day is

likely to think and behave differently from the citizen who
teaches school or the one who practices dentistry or the
one who runs a lathe or the citizen who drives a taxicab.
The hope is that each citizen will exercise his rights as a
citizen in good conscience, and that especially includes
businessmen because of their extended dynamic influence
upon civic affairs.

Decisions on the appropriate role of government in
our economy should be based on careful evaluations of the
degree of competition that exists, the extent to which the
free forces of the market-place can contribute to the naion's
well-being, the degree to which the private economy functions successfully in serving the common good and, finally,
the degree to which government participation in economic
affairs can be limited and still assure the optimum fulfillment of our economic objectives.

Highly polarized views that urge either leaving every-
thing to the private sector or insistence that the government must regulate or own and operate all economic enterprises serve little useful purpose. Neither of these extremes
is necessary or feasible. The issue of the proper scope of
the government's role does not lend itself to dichotomous
black or white answers. The challenge is primarily one of
achieving appropriate balances and mixes between both
public and private responsibilities and functions.

Just as the nature of competition differs greatly among
industries, so the economic impact of government differs
greatly from function to function and sector to sector. Also,
competition does well in some industries and on some issues but poorly in other industries and on other issues.
Like competition, government policies are far from perfect
and they by no means assure the ideal rates of economic
growth or price stability or conservation of scare resources
or a clean environment or an equitable distribution of the

abundance we have achieved or many other economic goals that most of us seek for the United States.

In some ways competition has the same or similar strengths and weaknesses as government. Competition is supposed to provide a means by which conflicting or adversary forces can influence the allocation of resources and shape the products or services that are produced and that determine the prices charged and profits earned. Competition can be harsh in that only the fittest tend to survive. Likewise, government economic policies and practices are presumably set through decision-making processes where adversary views and influences are given opportunities to have their impacts. Successes and failures can be observed and judged and changes can and are made in policies and implementation. The democratic process in politics allows the public to share in setting policies and judging performance just as the competitive process permits businesses to compete with each other, or labor and management to bargain effectively, or producers and consumers to test their strengths in the marketplace. Neither competition nor government's role in the economy is all good or all bad, not so much because concepts are wrong but because performances fall so short of what we seek and expect. If competition worked better there would be less need for governmental activities in economic areas. Perhaps it would be better to say there would be need for less governmental activities, because there will always be economic roles that government alone can perform.

We have already reviewed manifestations of notable progress made in our economy over the past half century. Also, we have observed that many serious and difficult problems still face us. We shall, hopefully, continue to make progress in solving or easing some of these problems and difficulties. Equally hopefully, our standards of per-

formance will be more and more demanding. Many gaps
between goals and performance will persist because our
goals will be more ambitious. Other gaps will arise as we
try to move toward a more perfect economic performance.
Such performance will always be elusive, but as we struggle
to achieve it, we certainly will make more progress.

The constructive government role in economic matters
depends on the successes and failures of the private sectors
as well as the character and quality of government. In the
Great Depression there was irresistable pressure on the
Federal Government to do something about the terrible
waste of unemployment and idle industries as well as the
terrible hardships Americans suffered. When conditions are
better there is somewhat less pressure for government action,
or at least a smaller portion of the population pushes for
new policies and new measures. Also, much legislation de-
rives from executive and legislative leadership so that a
concerned President and concerned Congressional leaders
will introduce new policies more than those who oppose
reform and change.

Clearly not all Congresses have the same composition
of brains or visions or judgments as to what is or is not in
the public interest. Some Congresses are more conservative
and some are more liberal; some are more innovative and
some are more traditional in their orientation; some are
more responsive to specific pressure groups and others are
more responsive to counter pressure groups; some are internationally oriented and some are domestically focused;
some lean toward labor and others toward business. The
same is true of the Executive Branch of government. Some
presidents and cabinet members and senior officials see
economic issues in a different light from other administra-
tions. This bothers many observers because they fear the
consequences of election results which bring changes in

party control that lead to different philosophical orientations.

Each of the two major political parties in the United States has different economic views. The Democratic members of the House and the Senate tend on the whole to be more liberal -- in the modern sense — than the Republicans. But there are many conservatives in the Democratic ranks, especially Southerners, and a number of liberals in the Republican ranks. The policy differences between the parties are not so tremendous as to result in rigid and unyielding stalemates when a President is from one party and a Congress is dominated by the other party. There is no hard party discipline in this country similar to many nations abroad where the parliamentary system prevails. So we manage to accommodate many diverse views and pressures. We move forward sometimes swiftly and sometimes slowly and we even move backwards occasionally. But, it is almost certain that the role of government will continue to be substantial no matter what the political complexion is in the Congress or in the White House. And the record will vary greatly.

I believe that the economic performance of the Nixon Administration over the past five years and one month has been the worst in a half century, if not longer. As noted, we are in Mr. Nixon's second recession and we had not come near full recovery before this decline began. We are in the midst of the worse peacetime inflation in this century and there is every indication prices will rise even faster in the months and perhaps in the years ahead. The dollar has been devalued twice and other currencies revalued in relation to the dollar. Our national debt has increased over one hundred billion dollars since Mr. Nixon took office in January 1969. We have had our first trade deficit in many decades. Interest rates have set new high records in this century. We have given up the war on inflation, on welfare reform, on slum clearance and we have abandoned the war on poverty. It is difficult to remember when our economic image and influence reached lower levels in international circles. Worst of all has been the erosion of confidence in public service and the pervasive sense of distrust. Great promises and poor deeds have undermined the national will and the nation's commitment to economic progress.

It is ironic that such a poor performance should have been forthcoming from almost fanatical devotees to marketplace economics. Haters of inflation have given us the worst dose of peacetime inflation we can remember. Another dire threat to our society, in the mind of President Nixon and his economists, was deficit financing and yet they gave us our biggest peacetime deficits. They accepted direct controls when the forces of inflation threatened to overwhelm us and after a period of some success in containing inflation they undermined controls and now we have rampant inflation.

One might ask whether this experience of recent years does not justify a retreat from reliance on public policy and greater dependence of competition. That does not make much sense in light of the miserable failures of these competition and free-market oriented economists. What is needed is a change in leadership and a change in commitments and a change in forthrightness and integrity. It is not a lesser role of government that we need but a better role. It need not be a larger role, but it must be more dedicated and more reliable. It must be related to performance and not words alone. And that also means improved deeds rather than just rhetoric in support of both competition and sound public policies.

Our economy needs broader and better competition

and we need excellence of conscience in guiding citizen actions towards better ways of living. Furthermore, we need a public-private mix which will preserve the best features of our private enterprise system and supplement that system's performance by adopting and implementing constructive public policies and practices. Unfortunately the economists now in the saddle have weakened the private as well as the public contributions and we will have to advance changes in leadership to make the system work more competently and confidently towards ever greater progress in the achievement of life's high values.

Lecture Two

by Luther H. Hodges

M. L. Seidman, for whom this distinguished Memorial
Town Hall Lecture Series is named, perceived in his lifetime the key responsibilities of business in a complex and
competitive world. And in his syndicated column on taxation which appeared in more than 100 newspapers all
over the United States, Mr. Seidman, a certified public
accountant, demonstrated his keen comprehension and
statesman-like approach to subjects that later became the
central theme of these lectures at Memphis State University.

Knowing of his wise counsel to presidents, to business
leaders and to the public, and recognizing the stature of
Seidman lecturers who have preceded me, it is a signal
honor to me to be invited to speak on this occasion.

Adhering to the main theme of the lecture series, of-
ficially entitled "The Social Conscience of American Business," I am selecting, on this occasion, a more specific
topic: "The Responsibility of American Business Toward
the Community."

Appeals to the conscience to be completely fair in

competitive conduct in the free marketplace have always been a complex and difficult exercise, even to men and women of highest ethical principles. Now, in 1974, the conflict between energy shortages and environmental snarls faces us; over-population and inflation; production dislocations and monetary difficulties; unemployment and the obligation to protect the civil rights of others; international insecurity and complicated governmental regulations and guidelines; all of these converge at this moment to challenge Americans — and chiefly business entrepreneurs and managers — with heretofore unmatched responsibilities. Abiding by the Golden Rule has never been easy, and circumstances in this day require an even more careful study of what must be done when we "do unto others as you will have them do unto you."

My premise, however, is that it was never more important, never more vitally necessary, never more urgent, that we find the way to live together in peace and with consideration for the rights of others— those others being our neighbors on both sides of the tracks, other business men and women, other Americans and other citizens of the world.

I was in active business with a large corporation for over thirty years. This experience was followed, just after World War II, by a public service stint in West Germany, as an administrator with the Marshall Plan Program, working with business and industry to rehabilitate West Germany. I was Lieutenant Governor and Governor of North Carolina. I served as U. S. Secretary of Commerce under Presidents John F. Kennedy and Lyndon Johnson and I now serve on several corporate boards.

In my personal and civic life, I have been active in the church, served as president of Rotary International, and have been intimiately associated with the University of North Carolina.

I cite these items of my biography, mainly in order to illustrate the attitudes that I invite you to consider in speaking of the social conscience of American business. I am reminded that James Thurber once said that although he wasn't the smartest man in the world, he'd "been through more" than the average man. So, I can say I say I have been through the inter-lacing labyrinths of business, government, and human relationships with people in all walks of life.

Accordingly, I feel a close relationship with this subject. I have for most of my business life felt strongly that business had, or should have, a business conscience. In fact, while I was Secretary of Commerce I wrote a book entitled *THE BUSINESS CONSCIENCE,* published by Prentice-Hall, Inc. and the royalties therefrom were assigned to the United Negro College Fund (USA) and to the Methodist Colleges of North Carolina.

It must be acknowledged that many people do not regard social conscience as a foremost attribute of the businessman. An opinion poll of this audience, or of Memphis State faculty and students — yes, even a national poll — would probably show that only a minority believe that business does possess a social conscience.

There are those who believe that business is ruthless, intent on profit above all else, and has little regard for the community's best interest.

I would differ with the majority. I hold that business *does* have a social conscience. Yet, I must admit that many cases can be shown of corporations and businesses that seem some of the time to demonstrate a paucity of social responsibility.

I believe that those occasional evidences of lack of

social conscience are exceptional to the general trend of good conduct towards the community of business. I assert this in spite of Watergate revelations and other examples of corruption in government and business. Yet, in our intricate society, we must marshal all of our efforts, all of what we recognize to be ethical principles and good will towards others, if we are to survive. Business also needs to monitor itself, and cooperate in businesswide monitoring processes.

One day, friends of mine in the textile business came to me, declared they were frustrated by government red tape and asked me for my help to get quick action.

They stated their "horror" case, and I asked, "Have you given me the whole story? Can I rely upon your figures?"

They assured me of the accuracy of their figures and the justice of their cause and I expedited their request through government channels.

Several years later at a cocktail party, I overhead the leader of the delegation say, "We sure bilked old Luther out of a million dollars that day, didn't we, fellows?"

My friends had lied to me. The lesson I learned is to be doubly careful when dealing with friends on government business. I should have been more wary and less trusting, and should have given more careful scrutiny to all "facts" and figures.

Another case of that kind occurred when I was Secretary of Commerce during the Kennedy Administration. Several companies in the electrical machinery industry had conspired to fix prices and rig bids on government contracts, and seven executives were sent to jail. I was encouraged by President Kennedy to draft a code of ethics for business. We invited 25 leading businessmen to come to Washington to consider what we called "Statement on Business Ethics and a Call for Action."

But the businessmen assembled threw cold water on the proposal. Such a code, they said, would give the public the impression that all business was unethical. My counter argument, then and now, is that codes of ethics are good, and that the majority of business must help to monitor the bad, the bad being for in the minority.

I thought then, and believe now, that we need codes of ethics for businesses — strong codes that show up the minority of unethical businessmen and show to the majority (as well as to the public) that breaches of codes of ethics are not condoned by the majority of our business leaders. Business affairs should be conducted with a maximum of probity and honor; action to assure that business ought to be undertaken in the full glare of publicity, not in secret.

To support my premise that over the almost two hundred years of American history business has become better — not worse — in its attitudes towards the community, and to exhibit one up-to-the-minute instance of positive concern for keeping the posture on that happy incline, I was pleased to read in a recent issue of the *Wall Street Journal* a full-page advertisement that was heralded by this headline: "Wanted: Business Leaders With the Courage and Faith to Support a Movement to Make American More Honest."

The content of the article that followed was to announce the expansion of a foundation named "American Viewpoint," organized fifty years ago, and now revitalized and moved from New York to Chapel Hill, North Carolina, dedicated to promoting better ethics in America. One of its main points is the need for codes of ethics.

Ivan Hill, president of American Viewpoint and a retired Louisiana and Chicago businessman and advertising executive, listed some reprehensible actions by institutions and people, denoting corruption and disregard for the public's good — including a $15 million dollar employee theft ring in the meat industry; kickbacks for public works; a thesis-writing organization that helps college students cheat their way to higher degrees; bank stockholders' making dubious loans to themselves; excessive shoplifting, causing markup in goods for sale in stores; and other instances of unethical conduct.

Mr. Hill says the heart of his program is practical application of the Golden Rule. He proposes to expose unethical conduct through the public news media — that is, launch a campaign to shine the spotlight of publicity on unethical practices. He advocates education in the schools to promote ethics in business and personal and public life. He appeals to business and professional organizations to establish codes of ethics, and urges that civic clubs "re-energize their codes of ethics."

Ivan Hill hopes, he says, "to debunk dishonesty, to make it unfashionable, to turn the guy who puts something over into a bum, not a hero."

The best part of the American Viewpoint Foundation effort is the realization that Hill and other men and women who are in business and have been in business are confident that something more can be done to the credit of business people.

Just as no honorable laboring man is punished for the misdeeds of a few corrupt labor leaders; just as dedicated scholars are not contaminated when a few college students cheat; just as young athletes are not tarnished because a few players take bribes; just as we should not condemn all policemen when a few of them are exposed for thievery — neither should businessmen be exempt, or try to exempt themselves from codes of conduct and proper publicity when a minority of businessmen are condemned by the majority of the business world.

Business and business management have changed drastically — and for the better, ethically speaking — in the last decade. Although some of the current stories of intrigue and lack of public or social responsibility catch the headlines, I feel strongly that our business is improving greatly in its social attitudes toward the community.

First of all, our corporate management organizational structure has changed. In earlier days, one man, usually the founder and the sole owner, ran things.

The present-day "boss" is generally a college-trained specialist, with intensive education and skills in business management or finance. The modern manager, or chairman-President, is a professional. Trained either in a collegiate school of business administration or in an executive management forum, he has been taught and has learned to see his job as a multi-faceted responsibility. He knows his public, especially his local community, and he anticipates and responds to the community's needs. He trains his immediate staff. If his corporation has branch plants, he trains his local managers. He develops and relies upon a competent public relations staff to keep his corporation in familiar touch with the community.

There are exceptions, of course, to this type of far-seeing organization man, and even where the corporate "set-up" is modern, it sometimes fails because of a different caliber of leader, or owing to a particular circumstance.

For instance, on Tuesday, April 10, 1962, the chairman of the U. S. Steel Corporation sought an emergency appointment with President Kennedy. Just three days before, on April 7, the United Steel Workers Union and representatives of the steel industry had signed an agreement whereby the unions were not to ask for an increase in wages, and fringe benefits were increased only slightly.

President Kennedy had urged industry and labor to keep down prices, and the union management contract was expected to prevent inflation.

But now, three days later, the chairman of U. S. Steel called on the President to give him advance notice that U. S. Steel was going to raise the price of the company's steel products by an average of 3.5 per cent. Other steel companies also announced price rises the same day.

The President, in a news conference, called the price increase "wholly unjustifiable and irresponsible defiance of the public interest" and said that industry officials had shown "utter contempt for their fellow citizens."

As Secretary of Commerce, I looked on the price increase as an anti-business move by a corporation that should know better — for three reasons:

1. The American people would be so antagonized that all business might lose favor in the public eye.
2. It might start a new round of inflation.
3. It encouraged those who contended that voluntary restraints are impractical, and that only compulsion and regulation will work.

U. S. Steel had no other choice but to back down in response to a national uproar.

My conclusion then, as now, is that it is the duty of business to conduct its affairs in a manner that does not deliberately thwart the achievement of broadly accepted national goals. I stress that incident of twelve years ago as an exception to the gradual improvement in business attitudes which has taken place.

Business and industry leaders are constantly improving their stance or attitude toward the public — be it in a local community, in a region, or in the whole nation.

One of the young leaders in a very large banking institution made a speech in 1974 on "The Business of Social Responsibility." He deplored damage to the environment and said it can no longer be tolerated. Nor should we tolerate misleading advertising. Minorities are no longer willing to live with second class opportunities, he also said. I quote him directly: "Businesses, like individuals, are free only to the extent that their activities blend with the common good."

His view is similar to that of other ethical business leaders who have expressed what may be summarized in these four "Ifs".

> If we have not provided equality of opportunity because of moral responsibility, let us do it because of the economic need to fill the vacancies in our plants, offices, and laboratories.
>
> If we have not solved environmental pollution problems as a matter of civic duty, let us act to protect the pure air and water supplies that industry must have.
>
> If we have not eased poverty out of consideration for human compassion, let us do so to expand the buying power we need to keep our economy going.
>
> If we have not dealt with urban blight to meet esthetic needs, let us tackle it to protect the productivity of our population centers.

An illustration from industry comes from the maker of informal apparel, Levi Strauss and Company of San Francisco. Known as the maker of Levi's, the company contributes 3 per cent of its net after taxes to carefully chosen social programs, as well as hiring from minority groups. The company does not suffer financially, but actually realizes expanded sales and profits.

As you can see from the Levi experience, one can be successful profitwise and still be "community minded."

A fairly recent development in the U.S.A., and to some extent among most industrial societies, is popularly referred to as "Envionmental Problems."

Those problems are important, complicated, and involve greater expense in the conduct of our lives by business, industry, government, citizens — you and me.

Extremists put most of the blame for polluting the environment on industry, but it belongs to all of us. Untold billions of dollars must be spent if our environmental defects are to be corrected. The public must eventually pay the bill. I'm not sure that John Q. Public has accepted this fact. Will it willingly pay the bill?

Each of you must ask yourself the question: "How am I doing? Do I pollute? Do I litter? What am I doing about this problem that is so personal?" There have been several experiences with prominent people who never dreamed that this matter affected them personally. How about you? Do you feel that only corporations have the full responsibility?

Are you one of those who objects to the pollution from lead laden gas but who refuses to buy low-lead gasoline?

If industry were responsible for paying the whole bill, it would go out of business. Then there would be little or no money to pay any bills, or to correct any past mistakes.

Business, to exist, must make a profit. Otherwise, it will not be able to do all the other things society demands.

T. V. Learson of I.B.M. is correct, in my opinion, when he says: "There are some things business can do voluntarily to clean its own house . . . partly because they know abuses of the environment will not be tolerated."

What success industry meets in striving towards fulfillment of its social and corporate responsibility may bring on other problems of an international nature. I believe it is generally agreed that our business ethics in the United States — competition, taxes paid, and the like — are cleaner, broader and more exacting than in many other industrial nations. As industry adds to its desire to be among "good citizens" because of environmental demands, demands that sometimes run counter to the new energy crisis and its perils, the burden and the contrast become, ironically, more difficult, more dangerous. I refer to the threat of what is called U. S. "Ethical Imperialism."

I have talked with Jack Behrman, one of my assistant secretaries in the Commerce Department, and have read his views on multi-national enterprise. I am in accord with his beliefs about the dangers of telling foreign countries how to run their businesses. More than that, we must be discreet in trying to transform the way people and governments in foreign lands manage their lives and institutions. This is appropriate, also, when American business has plants in foreign countries. Behrman pointed to instances of "tampering with the family structure of French Canadians, the racial laws of South Africa or the leisurely lunch-at-home tradition in Italy." Sometimes American business is urged to interfere with the way things are done in foreign lands — or else the American business located there may withdraw or exercise some kind of economic pressure. This, Jack Behrman refers to as "ethical imperialism."

What we in America ought to do, he says, is to behave in so ethical a manner that others will benefit by our example. He states: "It is difficult to export what we do not have ourselves. Our first task is to give proof of how our own ethically based economic system works. Having done so, it is likely that others will import and adapt it as suitable."

I would like to say that I favor the pressure being put on corporations to do an even better job in dealing with environmental problems, in aiding minority and handicapped groups, in helping colleges and universities (includ-

ing private and church-related ones), in becoming better
corporate citizens. In this context, business charts a course
which, I hope, will carry it safely through the destructive-
laden channel of an environmental Scylla as one force and
energy Charybdis as the other.

To maintain his equilibrium in the crosscurrents of
countervailing forces that exert an impact on his business,
today's corporate executive increasingly must rely on a
specialist — his public relations adviser.

Just as he values the counsel of his legal staff, his chief
accountant, his sales manager and his production chief, the
corporate president must invest adequately in skillful community relations and communications professionals.

Never before in our American history has it been more
important that business engage the services of qualified
public relations counselors —- men and women of integrity
who are not afraid to say "no" or "watch out" or "let's try
this" to the boss; public relations men and women whose
integrity and understanding of media and the community
are hallmarks of the practitioners' total abilities and per-
sonality functions.

It is an axiom in law that a man who represents himself
in court has a fool for a client. The same may be said for
the able professional specialist who tries to manage his
own public relations by himself. In the same context, the
physician who attempts to direct his own press and communications efforts may have less than effective public relations in the community. And in the safe vein, a business
leader who fails to utilize his public relations staff appro-
priately does a disservice to himself and his stockholders as
well as to the public and his customers. Those professionals
need professional help — assistance that the public relations
staff can render.

Businessmen must select the best public relations men they can find, and give ear to their counsel.

When I referred earlier to support of higher education, it was because I am aware of the crisis on campuses in making financial ends meet. In giving to colleges and universities, business and government should, and must — in these perilous times — set priorities, and these ought to be in the broad public interest and in the spirit of free enterprise and enlightened self-interest.

The New York Times in an editorial last December 16th, reminded its readers that in major times of crisis in American history, the nation has turned to the universities for help. What would it have done agriculturally and industrially without the land grant colleges? Franklin D. Roosevelt got his brain trust from the universities. In university laboratories the secrets of atomic energy were unlocked. Universities became a key factor in the World War II defense effort.

The *Times* stressed, by contrast, the plight of universities today — idling in many instances because of near-recessions, and fearful of losing more students and faculty in times of rising expenses and declining income — as the universities struggle for survival.

In devoting money and attention to the community, business ultimately profits and prospers by budgeting sufficient amounts for research — research of its own and research in universities where, perhaps, some of the solutions to our current problems may be solved; and we — business, government, civic organizations, the mass of people — can be further along the way in agreeing upon and aspiring to a higher social responsibility to the community.

When business and foundations and individuals donate to worthwhile institutions, such as colleges and universities, many have found that wise philanthropy challenges the giver to be selective. It is not characteristic of the American businessman to give away his stockholders' money recklessly but to do so guardedly.

Specifically, in considering money gifts to universities, business makes its decisions painstakingly. Recognizing that public institutions are supported primarily by tax dollars, and that private universities and church-related colleges (and now the community colleges) have varied sources of support — from foundations and alumni and congregations and people in local communities as well as tax concessions due all educational institutions — it is too simplistic for a business executive to say, "I pay taxes to public universities and schools; my personal and corporate gifts go to private colleges and universities."

There seems to be emerging the practical and necessary attitude that business must invest — in its donations and research budgets — in specific programs that seem to have the most potentiality for both short-run and long-term gains for the good of society. And these budgeted investments may be best given in some cases to private institutions and in other instances to public institutions. For example, business and foundations and government carefully choose where to put money in medical research, in business school professorships, in scholarships and innovative programs, in projects that will protect the environment, in ideas that will aid scientists in the search for new sources of energy (whether by fission, fusion, solarpower, or new discoveries), in agricultural research, in population control, in city and regional planning, and in many other areas of research where some universities (private and public) have won reputations for excellence in fact finding or some other achievement.

In your own science and engineering programs at Memphis State University, you have multiplied your effectiveness of expanded research and training in the public interest and in performance of specific tasks useful to your mid-South region. Your achievements have been equally noteworthy in business research and in computer technology.

In my own state, the North Carolina Research Triangle Institute is owned by three universities — two of them public and the other private — North Carolina State University, the University of North Carolina at Chapel Hill, and Duke University, which is private.

Their research potential and what they have accomplished are enormous assets to the region and nation, just as the potential and attainments inherent in your own structure and service at Memphis State University fully justify the continued financial support of business and government, for you have the capacity for returning many fold to business and to the taxpayers what they have invested.

Let me appeal to you, especially to the younger people here, not to be discouraged and cynical about society or our great country because of current happenings.

I still have great faith in America, in her political system and in her ability (proven so many times) to lick her problems and to move on to greater success. My faith was renewed by something that Norman Cousins wrote recently:

> Humans are not helpless. They have never been helpless. They have only been deflected or deceived or dispirited. This is not to say their history has not been pockmarked by failure. But failure is not the ultimate fact of life; it is an aspect of life in which transient or poor judgments play larger roles than they should. So long as people do not persuade themselves that they are creatures of failure; so long as they have a vision of life as it ought to be; so long as they can comprehend the full meaning and power of the unfettered mind —

so long as they can do all these things, they can look at the world and, beyond that, the universe with the sense that they can be unafraid of their fellow humans and can face choices not with dread but with great expectations.

In closing, let me review my main points:

In spite of occasional spasmodic illustrations of well-publicized unethical conduct by a minority in the business world, the main trend for the majority of business is towards higher standards and better intentions and actions toward the community.

The gradual improvement noted in business responsibility toward the community throughout American economic history must be continuously encouraged.

Codes of business conduct will help business to be constantly aware of its responsibilities. Voluntary and regu'atory processes must be monitored.

Present-day crises, and hazards that loom in the future because of the energy shortages, environmental problems and consumer demands, should and will impel business to be even more watchful and determined to display community responsibility.

Although a degree of government regulation is required in many aspects of business enterprise and competition, it is essential that industry lead, rather than be led, in voluntary programs to benefit the community.

Many businesses display responsible conduct in investing wisely in community betterment, including aid to colleges and universities.

In the current dilemmas about energy shortages, pollution, and kindred national problems, business and government should turn again to universities to help plan for the future.

To aid him in awareness of community relations responsibilities the corporate executive must rely on the professional help of his public relations adviser.

We must show the world that the American Free Enterprise system does work and can work elsewhere in the world — if we can demonstrate how well an ethically-based economic system contributes to the well-being of people and nations.

It is axiom in journalism that it is the man who bites the dog that makes news. The striking, the sensational, the exception to the rule, the minority action sometimes captures the public attention — more than the day-by-day record of ethical conduct and respect for the rights of others. That is why I say American business, despite setbacks, has improved over the scores of years of our history. Paraphasing the words of a best-selling phonograph record, voiced by a Canadian radio commentator, it's time for the world to take a look at the good America is accomplishing as the experiment in democracy and free enterprise approaches its bicentennial. We do not sweep our troubles under the rug — they are displayed in a showcase for all to see and for corrections to be made. For we must be doing something right. That "right" consists of rules, regulations, urging, monitoring and understanding that business must and does have a scrupulous social consciousness and responsibility towards the community.

Lecture Three

by Robert Metz

Thank You. I'm pleased that you have chosen me, a newspaper man to participate in this distinguished lecture series. In responding, I'm going to remember that my value to you will be in my capacity as a reporter — a reporter who is in contact with businessmen on the one hand and individuals on the other.

I know that this was a factor in the decision to ask me to speak: the fact that I can see what businessmen are doing in matters reflecting on their social consciousness and further that I am in a position to see how their social consciousness — or lack of it — sits with individuals, particularly individual shareholders.

I am afraid that I'm going to have to paint a fairly dark picture in the area in which I am most familiar. For it appears that insofar as some of the 30-million individual investors are concerned, corporations and their executives are regarded with suspicion: that the individual shareholder sometimes feels himself to be in the presence of a group, of distinguished-looking men who number in their ranks a few gifted and determined corporate muggers who slyly plan the individual investor's undoing: using the very laws that are designed to protect shareholders to carry out their missions of pillage.

I'm going to suggest that the entire system suffers when this sort of thing is allowed to happen; I am going to suggest further that it is a proper role for the businessman to actively seek better laws to prevent the rip-off of the individual investor and to restore a greater measure of faith to our system.

Basically, I feel that some businessmen have lost the power to distinguish between right and wrong. I feel that some businessmen tend to approach their role in this light: "If it is profitable — and we can get away with it — it must be right."

Now that attitude is dangerous — especially so when it is evidenced in businessmen who are at the top of the heap, for the consumer assumes that if the top dogs do it, then surely it must be done at all levels of business. Business, in short, must be permeated with chicanery and cannot be trusted.

I wish to illustrate this point in a variety of ways — including the all-important medium of advertising, which as much as anything else, I think, sets the moral tone of business.

But first let me say that I think it would be naive to assume that we would ever reach a point of scrupulously correct advertising. In our capitalistic society I doubt that any business could succeed for long by constantly emphasizing that its competitor made a better product. Anyway, I suspect that most businessmen honestly believe that they deliver fine products and services whatever the facts may be.

But it is one thing to puff a product — to say that

the automobile you manufacture or your soap product is the finest money can buy. It is clearly lying to claim properties for a product that it does not have.

There are corporations — giant corporations — that seem to believe that it is all right to tell the consumer anything so long as the message is reasonable in tone. Never mind that the message is untruthful — so long as there is no way to hold the corporation responsible.

Let's go back in our mind's eye, then, to the days when the energy crisis was full blown. I was surprised to read an item on the front page of *The New York Times* in which top executives of major oil companies admitted that all gasoline of the same octane rating is "fungible".

You Memphis people — like myself, an Indiana boy — are familiar with farm terms. You probably know that a fungible is of such a nature or kind that one unit or part may be exchanged or substituted for another equivalent unit or part in the discharge of an obligation. Grain is a fungible and so is money. Any five dollar bill will serve to satisfy any five dollar debt.

Any five tons of a particular grade of winter wheat will satisfy a futures contract for five tons at that particular grade of winter wheat.

And we learn from the pages of *The New York Times* — from the very lips of top oil company executives that 5000 gallons of 100 octane fuel is the equivalent of any other 5000 gallons of 100 octane fuel

In fact, the executives went further, saying that when one major supplier was short of fuel *before* the shortage, that supplier could obtain fuel from a competitor to fill the gap. On first blush that seems to show an admirable spirit of cooperation between executives of rival corporations in a fiercely competitive industry, and it is indeed admirable. There is only one catch.

Several of the giant oil companies spend millions of dollars each year telling the individual consumer why their particular brand of gasoline is superior to all the others.

One major refiner's gasoline is said to contain detergents that will cleanse the motorist's engine — making it run longer without major repair or overhaul.

Another major refiner's product gets greater mileage — bursts through a paper target miles down the road from the spots where identical cars burning competitors fuel have run out of gas.

Still another major refiner's product contains a specific element that contributes to engine life. In this case, the accent is not on a clean engine but on reduced repair costs due to the action of the specific chemical element.

Now then, if the refiners rely on these appeals to bring the customer in, then it seems to me that the customer has every right to expect that he will get the product he comes for. If the refiner, however, in his dealings with other refiners treats his product as a fungible — freely exchanging his fuel for fuel of equal octane depending on who is short at a given moment in history — then the refiner has no right to advertise his fuel as different from the others. This is dishonest — or so it seems to me.

There can be negative consequences in this dishonesty. Suppose, for example, that a motorcyclist comes into a station which advertises long mileage and due to a refiner's swap his tank is instead filled with a gasoline with that specific element the other refiner puts in for prolonged engine life.

Now motorcycle mechanics believe that the particular element in question fouls the sparkplugs of the increasingly popular two-stroke engines used on most trail bikes.

Some of these trail bikes and many other two-stroke motorcycles are widely used on the highways. If the harmful element in the gasoline causes the motorcycle to sputter and stall on the highway it is easy to imagine the possibility of injury or even death for the rider overtaken by a car or truck.

I am using this offbeat example to indicate that advertising one product and delivering another supposedly similar product can be dangerous.

It is certainly dishonest and cynical. When the consumer realizes this kind of thing is being done, he is further disillusioned in an age of disillusionment. Watergate becomes a broader concept signifying a rip-off in commerce as well as government.

Obviously, I was bothered by this disclosure that gasoline is treated as a fungible — is transferred freely among refiners — despite powerful advertising that seeks to prove that there are definite and important distinctions.

By coincidence, I had occasion to discuss the matter almost immediately thereafter with people in a position to confirm the situation. At a lunch in *The New York Times* dining room I and several other reporters and editors met with a former director of one of the world's largest oil companies and a former officer of a leading midwestern oil company. There were also a couple of leading Wall Street oil analysts at the lunch.

When I suggested that it was dishonest to treat gasoline as a fungible in view of the advertising campaigns and some very real differences and further suggested that this added to the corporate credibility gap, journalist and oil man alike smiled and said that all advertising was dishonest.

I argued to no avail that it was possible to advertise gasoline honestly and cited more than one example. For instance, Jean Paul Getty, who understands the appeal of price if anyone does, has set up his gasoline stations as marketeers of premium gasoline only. Benefitting, I assume, from the economies implicit in handling one kind of fuel only, he advertises that he will sell premium fuel at a discount from premium fuel prices.

At this meeting of journalists and oil men, all agreed that the Getty advertising *was* honest. They wouldn't all agree, however, that the admittedly dishonest advertising by other majors was reprehensible.

I submit that as the consumer begins to share the cynicism of these oil men and journalists, something is lost to the entire business community. Credibility in general suffers and, bringing the point back to my main theme, ultimately fewer investors trust stocks as a refuge from inflation and as a means of participating in the growth of the economy.

Now let's pursue this question of corporate credibility and honesty into the field of public relations, advertising's first cousin. I'm going to give you just a single example of the way giant corporations sometimes use public relations to mislead and indeed mislead to the extent that they actually present their cases unfairly, in my opinion.

I'm thinking about a press release sent out by the Great Atlantic and Pacific Tea Company a year or so ago. The thrust of this press release, an earnings statement, was that things were much improved for the long-troubled super market operator. That indeed operating losses were being reduced so effectively that profitable operations were just around the corner.

Specifically, the company said that losses in the latest quarter had been cut impressively from the quarter before that, true enough. But the A & P people knew that newspapers that have the staff to do so will analyse earnings statements such as these and seek out a different, standard comparison. They will take a company's earnings for the latest quarter and compare them with the earnings in the comparable quarter in the prior year.

That way, seasonal factors can be eliminated from consideration. A look at the records showed that the A & P had lost more money in the latest quarter than in the comparable quarter in the prior year.

But the stunning news for the A & P was buried several paragraphs down in the release. It was so far down, I suspect, that some newspapers with limited space for earnings reports may not have printed the information.

This was the fact that the A & P, a company with a record of continuous dividends, quarter by quarter, that stretched all the way back to 1924, was eliminating the payout in the latest quarter.

Now the A & P managed to report a small profit two quarters later: then fell into the red again in the August quarter of 1973, then reported a 3-cent-a-share profit in its November quarter of 1973. Its overall result for those three quarters combined was still a deficit, though the company again declared a dividend of 15 cents a share, payable next month.

The point of course is that you can always sugarcoat the pill but there is always the risk that you may overdose the patient.

When great corporations like the A & P use the press release weapon in this manner, shareholders once again are turned against business generally in my opinion and if investors don't trust you, they won't buy your stock.

There are more subtle tricks that are used to keep investors buying stocks of companies with fading fortunes. Many a growth company in the late 1960s managed to show one quarter after another of ever increasing profits and this continued in some cases for years. Then suddenly came the massive write-offs of perhaps hundreds of millions of dollars in ventures gone awry. Stocks of such companies plummeted sharply in price overnight as a result of massive institutional selling.

It suddenly turned out that a company's planned schedule of growth was actually a question of *adjusting* income statements to give the illusion of growth at the expense of shareholders attracted to such situations.

Now the last great Wall Street game of growth ended in 1969 as investors became more and more disillusioned with corporations and their mealy-mouthed statements about profits growth generally.

Certainly Wall Street was more at fault even than the corporations themselves in propagating this false faith in "growth". Brokerage firms fell all over each other hiring "big producers" — salesmen who would or could deliver commission business to the firm at any cost.

I won't bore you with the final results of this irresponsible period in Wall Street history. You are all aware that the business shrank drastically — especially the retail business: that is the business of selling stocks to individuals.

Major brokerage houses went under and others had to be merged out of existence to keep Wall Street itself from being swallowed up in a crisis of confidence similar to that which hit the nation's major banks back in the 1930s.

In their defense, the Wall Street community did act responsibly in using millions of dollars that had been set aside to build a new headquarters for the New York Stock Exchange to settle accounts of brokerage house customers who were threatened with losses when their brokers went out of business.

Now the formula was one of long standing and for many years the New York Stock Exchange had taken pride in its record of safety to the assets left with its member firms.

As long as ten years ago, during the famous salad oil scandal which caused two major firms to go under, the exchange made good the debts of the two brokerage houses.

Investors were thus led to believe that deposits of cash or stock left with a member firm were as safe as those left in the banks. While many were disillusioned with the basic soundness of Wall Street in the crisis of 1970, the Exchange nevertheless used its millions to keep the securities ship afloat. But the formula by which customers are protected has since been changed for the worst.

With Wall Street coaching, Congress passed the Securities Investor Protection Act, setting up an organization to handle the cases of investors whose funds and securities were left with brokerage houses that failed.

At first, it seemed quite clear that investors would be protected as fully as depositors in banks that had federal deposit insurance protection. The surety limits were as high or higher under S.I.P.C. and everyone waited in confidence thinking that when a brokerage firm failed, everyone would be made whole.

But when the major firm of Weis Securities went under, it quickly became apparent that the investing public had been ripped off again. Instead of seeing to it that the customers' securities were transferred to another broker in sound financial circumstances — the technique that worked so well in past debacles — accounts were settled under S.I.P.C. led to more investor dismay.

The major banks, acting quite sensibly and in the only way they could under the circumstances, promptly sold securities Weis had pledged to cover its loans. The prices the banks received were low. The indiscriminate dumping severely depressed the markets for the shares in question. The owners of those shares were powerless to remedy the situation even with the deposit of additional funds. The shares were sold at once — willy-nilly and without contact with the owners to see what they wanted done.

Others, whose shares were held in the vaults of the bankrupt firm, learned that they would be unable to take. action to sell their shares for many weeks. Not unexpectedly, the Weis failure came at a time of falling stock prices when the collateral backing brokerage house capital positions erodes rapidly.

It is very clear, then, that one of the first orders of business if the individual investor is to have his faith in Wall Street restored is to improve S.I.P.C. so that the customer will be assured that his ability to trade shares will never be impaired by the weakness or failure of his broker.

Yet there is no sign that those in the best position to do something about investor protection are interested. I had a conversation with a leading Wall Streeter just this week about shareholder protection and his chief response to the suggestion that S.I.P.C. was a failure was that it had done its job by assuring that the failure of one brokerage house would not cause the failure of one or more other brokerage houses. Without S.I.P.C. there was always the danger of a domino effect since there are always millions of dollars worth of securities belonging to one brokerage house in the hands of dozens of others.

The brokerage community, it seems to me, has clearly missed the message of the Sol Seidman Case. Mr. Seidman (no relation to P. K. Seidman), a small businessman in the export trade had invested wisely years ago, buying the shares of American Home Products. By adding to his position over the years he managed to accumulate shares worth well over a half a million dollars. The shares represented the bulk of Mr. Seidman's wealth. He was, in short, the embodiment of the investor's dream. That by carefully selecting the shares of some fine company and holding onto them that one might be able to buy financial security in an insecure world. The story is rich with irony.

Mr. Seidman was a Weis customer. When that firm failed it looked as though Mr. Seidman was in the clear. In an eleventh hour effort to save the firm, the New York Stock Exchange had encouraged the transfer of some accounts to other more viable brokerage houses. The Exchange chose the larger accounts for this switch in making the suggestion since a lot could be accomplished with relatively little action.

Indeed, Mr. Seidman's shares had been transferred to that paragon of Wall Street virtue, Merrill Lynch, Pierce, Fenner & Smith. However, as it turned out, American Home Products had been in the midst of a distribution of shares under a 3 for one stock split at the time of the Weis failure.

The old American Home Product shares were transferred to Merrill Lynch and the new shares, were lost to Mr. Seidman under the peculiar workings of the federal legislation. The shares were sold and he was handed a check for $50,000 and a right to sue. He thus had only one-third of his American Home Products capital at Merrill.

Worse yet, Merrill discovered that Mr. Seidman was under margined on the basis of the one-third holding and his shares were sold to satisfy his margin debt.

Not only was Mr. Seidman thus left with his law suit, he also owed a tax bill on the capital gains which he was assumed to have earned on the sale of the American Home Products shares.

If S.I.P.C. is successful legislation, you will never convince Sol Seidman — or any of millions of readers of *The New York Times* and other publications that carried his

story. And there are the stories of other Weis customers
who were delayed for weeks while the firm was wound up.
In some cases this resulted in losses of equity in homes
customers of Weis had made commitments to buy. Elderly
investors were deprived of dividends indefinitely. The telling of these stories further helped disillusion the investor.

And yet, months after the debacle at Weis, a prominent
Wall Street figure can comment to a reporter that the legislation has worked because it does not allow Wall Street to
die in a death struggle with the dominos. I learned just
this week that a task force is grappling with the weaknesses
in the law but early action is not expected.

I suggest to you that Wall Street can also be nibbled
to death. It can be nibbled to death through the cynicism
engendered by blatantly dishonest advertising: it can be
nibbled to death through the cynicism engendered by the
publishing of misleading press releases and by the hyping
of earnings through accounting tricks. And it can be nibbled
to death by the sheer apathy and withdrawal of the man
who built the edifice in the first place — the individual
investor who puts his money in the Street to help build this
capitalistic society.

I suggest to you that corporations have neglected to
meet their responsibilities as citizens and are not yet sufficiently socially conscious.

Consider this fact: the latest issue of *U. S. News &
World Report* has the results of a survey of 500 American
leaders regarding the most influential men in the United
States today. Fourth on the list — after the President, Henry
Kissinger, and George Meany in that order — is none other
than Ralph Nader who is described as the "watchdog of
government and industry for the common man".

Thus it seems clear, that the leaders of this nation
recognize that Ralph Nader in his sometimes poorly-

documented attacks has had an enormous impact on the nation's thinking: that he has struck a responsive note with millions of individual Americans and investors.

But what have the corporations done to counter this: What has Wall Street done? Certainly not enough. Contrary to what you might think, I am not suggesting that corporations become paragons; that we move into a society of impeccable morality. Rather I am suggesting that if corporate responsibility is not elevated there will be further lack of trust: further erosion of confidence in markets and products.

A broker with a moralistic outlook said to me recently that in the old days on Wall Street the emphasis was on credit for which he said one could read the word trust. Today we speak of credibility. People are more concerned with the question of whether they will be believed than with the basic idea of simply telling the truth.

In conclusion, I am reminded of the story I love to tell about the gorilla who entered a bar and ordered a martini. With that he laid a hundred dollar bill on the bar and waited. The bartender said, "Yes sir?" and nervously walked down to the end of the bar to confer with the manager.

"That gorilla just gave me a hundred dollar bill for a martini. What'll I do," he asked?

"Give him fifty cents change. Gorillas can't count," said the manager.

So the bartender went back, mixed the martini and carefully set it before the gorilla; picking up the one hundred dollar bill. He then walked to the cash register, rang up the sale and pulled a fifty-cent piece out of the cash register. He laid the coin before the gorilla who just stared at it — real hard.

The bartender began to get nervous and tried to

strike up a conversation. "Ah, we don't see many gorillas in here", he said to the gorilla.

The gorilla muttered: "At ninety-nine fifty a drink, it's no wonder!"

Now it seems to me that for too long some businessmen — corporate executives, brokers and what have you — have treated the individual like that gorilla. Sell him what you have and make him pay through the nose. If he complains, don't worry, there is nothing we can do about it. But the American public is like a monster when sufficiently riled. It will certainly fight back in time — if it doesn't simply go into the woods and refuse to come back to the market place at all. Thank you.